ACKNOWLEDGEMENTS

I thank God first and foremost for laying it on my heart to write *Whoo's In The Boat*.

I am grateful to have had parents who saw to it that my sister and I were raised in a loving, Christian home. My mom and dad encouraged me to chase my dreams, no matter what they may be, as long as God is at the helm.

Thank you to my own family, friends, teachers and mentors who have encouraged me in so many ways throughout my journey. And a special thanks to my kids; Haylie, Harrison, WT, Shelby, and Matt, who always keep me laughing and young at heart.

I would like to add a special note of gratitude to my daughter, Haylie, who not only assisted in editing but also contributed some insight and point of view.

Many thanks to John Goldsmith, for lending his expertise and time.

Also, Zack Orsborn, thank you for guiding me through my first book.

ABOUT THE AUTHOR

Lisa Brubaker Burch grew up in Memphis, Tennessee and currently resides in Mississippi. While pursuing a career in nursing, Lisa worked as a daycare instructor and kindergarten assistant teacher at St. Luke United Methodist. She also has taught in various children's programs including Sunday school, vacation bible school, and gymnastics. As a critical care nurse she served as a patient caregiver, educator, and team leader. Later she conducted cardiac research studies at Memphis Heart Clinic which led to her current occupation as a health and wellness instructor. She has a passion for assisting others to a better life mentally, physically, and most importantly, spiritually.

ABOUT THE ILLUSTRATOR

Kristi Goldsmith grew up in a family that always encouraged her to pursue her artistic passions. She studied fashion at Stephens College in Columbia, Missouri, and fine art at the Art Academy of the University of Memphis. When her dear friend, Lisa Burch, wrote *Whoo's In The Boat*, Kristi knew she wanted to contribute to the project because it spoke to her artistic creativity and resonated with her religious upbringing. Kristi maintains a close relationship with God and is eager to help children establish their own relationships with Him.

INTRODUCTION

Clouds drift by one by one, sometimes vibrant with color and sometimes dark and stormy. A beautiful picture is formed as they mesh together; one painted by the finger of God Himself. I liken this to one's life. The seasons and events are playing a role in God's final masterpiece, His grand purpose for our lives.

It was 2020 when the world seemed to be spinning out of control. One early morning I walked out to meet with God and as I looked up at the beautiful stars I thought, "This earth is like a storm tossed ship rocking to and fro." A childhood song came to mind: "He's got the whole world in His hands…" I said to the Lord, "You do have us and you are at the helm." As I opened His word and began to read, I started to see verses leap out at me. Verses pertaining to the wind and the waves, the light and the anchor, and so much more. This vivid imagery coupled with a desire to spread God's word inspired me to write a children's book.

Jesus said "Permit the children to come to me; do not hinder them; for the kingdom of God belongs to such as these. Truly I say to you, whoever does not receive the kingdom of God like a child will not enter it at all" (Luke 18:16-17).

My hope is that this little book will encourage our children to look toward the Father, as well as rekindle the childlike spirit in you, so that your light will shine like the stars of heaven.

A watercolor by Bonnie (Bees) Burch, my mother-in-law who captured this special moment of my daughter Haylie and me on the shores of Destin. Thank you for the treasured times spent in your art loft overlooking the emerald green waters of the Gulf of Mexico.

DEDICATION

I would like to dedicate my first children's book to a few organizations that are dear to me:

Timothy Hill Children's Ranch
Christian Relief Fund
Youth Villages

And in honor of all the children of the world.

The harbor was buzzing with excitement as the local fishermen prepared for the day's catch. Fishing was the livelihood of the village. Everyday Jody watched the fishermen head out through the pass to the sea and waited for them to return to the harbor. He loved seeing all the fish of every shape and size and color, and dreamed of being a fisherman himself one day. But Jody also wanted to be a fisher of men. Jody loved Jesus and wanted others to love Jesus, too. He had dreams of traveling the seas, to islands near and far, sharing the news of Jesus' love with all of the children he encountered along the way.

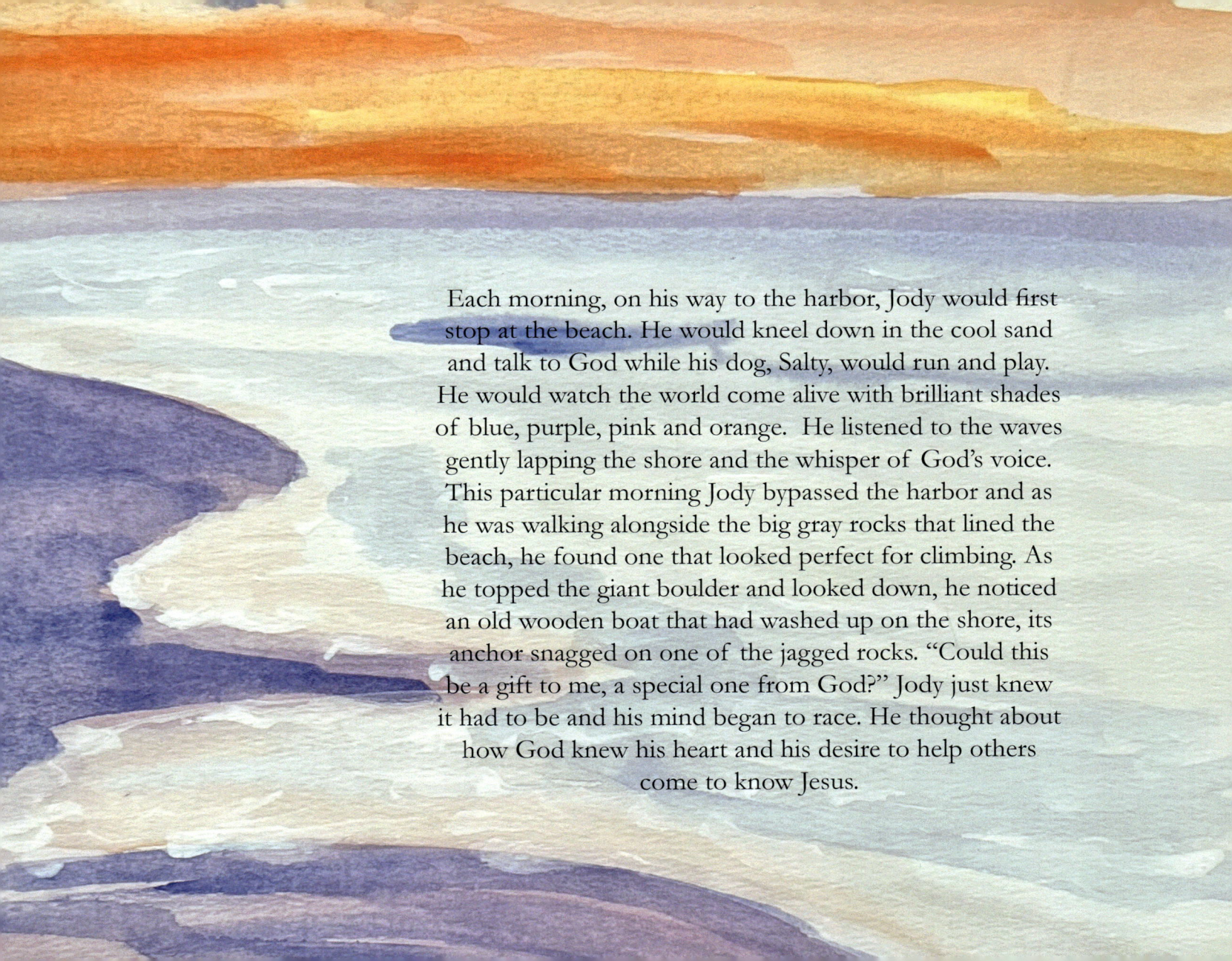

Each morning, on his way to the harbor, Jody would first stop at the beach. He would kneel down in the cool sand and talk to God while his dog, Salty, would run and play. He would watch the world come alive with brilliant shades of blue, purple, pink and orange. He listened to the waves gently lapping the shore and the whisper of God's voice. This particular morning Jody bypassed the harbor and as he was walking alongside the big gray rocks that lined the beach, he found one that looked perfect for climbing. As he topped the giant boulder and looked down, he noticed an old wooden boat that had washed up on the shore, its anchor snagged on one of the jagged rocks. "Could this be a gift to me, a special one from God?" Jody just knew it had to be and his mind began to race. He thought about how God knew his heart and his desire to help others come to know Jesus.

"Salty dog, we need to get busy! I will replace her boards and give her a name!" Jody grabbed his hammer and nails and got straight to work. Last, he painted the name Happy on the stern.

Now all he needed was a captain. Who would be willing to brave such a voyage in a small, wooden old boat?

"Jody, I am Your Captain. My spirit and wisdom will be your inner compass and my word, The Captain's Log, will be a lamp to light the way."

Jody knew this could only be one thing, the voice of God!

Jody grabbed the essentials along with a little wooden treasure chest and his two best friends: Salty the dog and Good, an old wise owl. Good the owl would give a loud "HOOT!" every time Jody gleaned a bit of wisdom from God. He called these little lessons God kisses.

The ocean tides changed as the morning sun dawned red, a signal that it was time to set out into uncharted waters. As Jody pushed off he sang, "He's got the whole world in his hands, He's got you and me Salty in His hands, He's got you and me Good in his hands…"

After a long day of sailing, Jody felt his eyes start to get heavy. The sound of the waves and the gentle rocking of the boat soon lulled Jody to sleep.

Jody awakened to a thick fog. The sky and sea grew dark. Even the moon and stars were hidden from view. He began searching frantically for his lantern. Once he had it in hand he shined the dim light out upon the black water. Something resembling the sail of a boat floated by, until Jody realized, it wasn't a sail, it was a shark! The shark began to circle as the little boat rocked back and forth with the waves.

Lightning clacked the sky and the thunder boomed, echoing across the dark waves. Jody's boat tossed and pitched amongst the raging storm, threatening to capsize at any moment. Looking at his crew, Jody saw that he wasn't the only nervous sailor on this vessel. Salty dog looked cold and scared, shivering in the spray of the crashing waves, and Good owl hooted anxiously from his perch, tracking the massive shark with his feathery swiveling head. The shark nudged the stern of the boat with its brutish snout, and the crew trembled.
The vast sea made Jody feel so powerless.

Jody knew the only thing he could do right then and there was ask to God to keep Salty, Good owl, and himself safe in this moment of adversity. As Jody began to pray he heard a voice tell the hungry shark to disappear, and soon the ripping wind and wild waves became still.
"Was that Jesus in the boat?" he asked Salty and Good owl.

The rest of the night Jody sang songs and counted his blessings, which turned out to be a great way to pass the many hours he would still have to endure before making his first stop.

The morning light gave way to something glistening on the water…

"Look at all the dolphins!" shouted Jody with excitement.

Before long, the pod of dolphins began to put on a show. They were singing and dancing on the waves, their bellies pink with joy.

But wait, one dolphin was like nothing he had ever seen. There were shimmers and sparkles of every color of the rainbow on this dolphin's belly.

"Hi, I'm Harmony," she sang out, as she lifted her head at the bow of the boat.

"Can I help you on your journey?
Dolphins are the best helpers you know…we are very smart and love children!"

"That would be wonderful!" Jody replied.

Just like that, they were on course with Harmony the dolphin leading the way.

Pretty soon the island that Harmony was aiming toward came into view. Children of all ages were laughing and playing in the sand and splashing in the tide pools. One by one they spotted the boat, and they all gathered on the shore to greet Jody and his crew.

"Boats always bring gifts!" The children thought, as they jumped
up and down with anticipation.

They stood in awe as Jody stepped out of his boat with Good owl and Salty dog. "That is just a little boy…" they whispered.

"I have a gift for you!" Jody exclaimed. "It is a special gift, one that lasts forever!"
"What kind of gift could that be?" they wondered. Jody decided to show them love so that they would know God and his Son, Jesus, because God is love. Jody also gave them handmade gifts as well, and while he made the gifts he would sing, "This little Christian light of mine, I'm gonna let it shine, let it shine all the time, let it shine."

Jody made little boats out of coconuts, beautifully strung necklaces of pearly shells, and balls full of phosphorous plants from the sea that would glow when they bounced. He made jungle gyms out of bamboo and vines to climb and swing on. He painted vibrant murals on jetty rocks, using colorful berries as paint.

Harmony gave piggy back rides to the children, gently gliding through the water as they cheered with joy. She would blow colorful bubbles and do flips and jumps and all kinds of dolphin tricks. It was all so magical.

At night the children would sit around the crackling fire with Good owl and Salty, surrounded by a million stars. They would share fresh papayas and mango along with sweet coconut milk. Jody taught them songs and read stories about living water and the bread of life from the Bible, The Captain's Log. They began to see the Love of Jesus through Jody.

Jody told them about how God sent his only son Jesus, and that whoever believes in Him will have everlasting life. Jody explained how God's love brings us good gifts such as joy, grace, peace, protection, and so much more. The children then understood what Jody meant when he said he would give them a gift that would last forever.

"Hoot!" exclaimed Good the owl.

When it was time for Jody to head back home, he pulled one of the children to the side and told him "Cotie, you have become one of my good friends. I am going to count on you and Harmony to keep the love light of Jesus going."

He reminded them to stand on the Rock and to always hold on to hope.

"Storms will come and go, so watch for the pretty rainbows on the other side, because God will always keep His promises."

Cotie assured him that with the help of Harmony, all the children would surely not forget Jody, Salty, Good, and the everlasting gift that they shared with the island.

The children all stood at the edge of the water and waved goodbye until the little boat disappeared from view.

The glow of a lighthouse was in the distance, safely guiding the little crew in the direction of the harbor. Upon arrival, Jody, Salty, and Good owl disembarked and Jody double knotted the ropes to the dock, making sure Happy was secure.

As Jody began to unload the boat, he noticed that his treasure box was heavier. When he opened it he saw that the children had carefully packed beautiful gifts for Jody without him even realizing it. Jody was in awe of what he saw: wind chimes of bamboo and shells, precious gems of all colors, island spices, perfumes and oils. All reminders of the things that Jody had done for them. The blessings and love he gave away came back to him.

Soon all the fishermen on the harbor stopped what they were doing and gathered around Jody to listen to the stories of his journey. They couldn't believe what this little boy had accomplished.

The sun was setting over the harbor and the sky was bursting with color. Taking a seat aboard Happy, Jody kicked back, propped his feet up and watched the stars pop out one by one. He noticed two stars close together that looked like two eyes gazing back at him. One quickly disappeared as if God was winking at him.

With a big smile on his face Jody tipped the brim of his hat over his eyes. Salty dog stretched out beside him and Good owl perched on the bow of the boat.
As Jody closed his eyes and thought back over his adventure, he remembered the beautiful flowers and the rainforest, the wild animals and the fireflies that seemed to light up the whole island. But most of all he could hear the sounds of the children laughing on the beach and singing the songs that Jody had taught them. He imagined that God was tapping along to those sweet voices and smiling down on His beautiful creation.

"Hey Good, Salty, you know what? Jesus WAS in the boat the whole time!"

Good owl gave a loud "HOOT!" and Jody drifted off to sleep…

CAPTAIN'S LOG

For God so loved the world, that he gave His only begotten Son, that whoever believes in Him shall not perish, but have eternal life. John 3:16 NASV

Go therefore and make disciples of all the nations, baptizing them in the name of the Father and the Son and the Holy Spirit. Matthew 28:19 NASV

And he said to them, "Follow Me, and I will make you fishers of men." Matthew 4:19 NASV

Wait for the Lord; Be strong and let your heart take courage; Yes wait for the Lord. Psalm 27:14 NASV

Yet those who wait for the Lord will gain new strength; they will mount up with wings like eagles, they will run and not get tired, they will walk and not become weary. Isiah 40:31 NASV

Every good thing given and every perfect gift is from above, coming down from the Father of lights, with whom there is no variation or shifting shadow. James 1:17 NASV

The joy of the Lord is your strength. Nehemiah 8:10 NASV

Trust in the Lord with all your heart and do not lean on your own understanding. In all your ways acknowledge Him, and he will make your paths straight. Proverbs 3:5-6 NASV

I will instruct you and teach you in the way which you should go; I will counsel you with My eye upon you. Psalm 32:8 NASV

Be strong and courageous, do not be afraid or tremble at them, for the Lord your God is the one who goes with you. He will not fail you or forsake you. Deuteronomy 31:6 NASV

Your word is a lamp to my feet and a light to my path. Psalm 119:105 NASV

And he got up and rebuked the wind and said to the sea, "Hush, be still." And the wind died down and it became perfectly calm. Mark 4:39 NASV

For I know the plans I have for you, declares the Lord, plans for welfare and not for calamity to give you a future and a hope. Jeremiah 29:11 NASV

Let them praise the name of the Lord, for His name alone is exalted; His glory is above earth and heaven. Psalm 148:13 NASV

How blessed are the people who know the joyful sound! O Lord, they walk in the light of Your countenance. Psalm 89:15 NASV

I am the living bread that came down out of heaven; if anyone eats of this bread, he will live forever; and the bread also which I give for the life of the world is My flesh. John 6:51 NASV

How precious also are your thoughts to me, O God! How vast is the sum of them! Psalm 139:17 NASV

The Lord your God is in your midst, a victorious warrior. He will exult over you with joy, He will be quiet in His love, He will rejoice over you with shouts of joy… Zephaniah 3:17 NASV

You alone are the Lord. You have made the heaven, the heaven of heavens with all their hosts, the earth and all that is on it, The seas and all that is in them. You give life to all of them, and the heavenly hosts bow down before you. Nehemiah 9:6 NASV

The steadfast of mind You will keep in perfect peace, because he trusts in You. Trust in the Lord forever, for in God the Lord we have an everlasting Rock. Isaiah 26:3-4 NASV

The Lord is good to all, and His mercies are over all His works. Psalm 145:9 NASV

For I am confident of this very thing, that He who began a good work in you will perfect it until the day of Christ Jesus. Philippians 1:6 NASV

Now may the God of hope fill you with all joy and peace in believing, so that you will abound in hope by the power of the Holy Spirit. Romans 15:13 NASV

I can do all things through Him who strengthens me. Philippians 4:13 NASV

But Jesus called them saying "Permit the children to come to Me, and do not hinder them, for the kingdom of God belongs to such as these..." Luke 18:16 NASV

But he must ask in Faith without any doubting, for the one who doubts is like the surf of the sea, driven and tossed by the wind. James 1:6 NASV

Let us hold fast the confession of our hope without wavering, for He who promised is faithful; and let us consider how to stimulate one another to love and good deeds... Hebrews 10:23-24 NASV